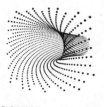

FIRSTMATTERPRESS

Portland, Ore.

CONSIDER
THE BODY,
WINGED

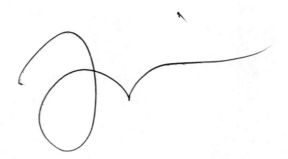

CONSIDER THE BODY, WINGED

jessica e. pierce

FIRSTMATTERPRESS

Portland, Ore.

First Edition

Published in the United States
by First Matter Press
Portland, Oregon

Paperback ISBN 978-1-7338246-5-1

Edited by Caroline Wilcox Reul,
Lauren Paredes, Andra Vltavín & Ash Good

Cover Illustration
Copyright © 2021 by Aleksandra Apocalisse
apocalisseart.com

Book design by Ash Good
ashgood.com

For my nine-year-old self:
thank you for being brave enough to say, *I am a poet*.
Here is our first book.
I love you.

POEMS

What do we know of endings?

—for Bevin

And if the earth could gather up all
it contains, all its clouded greened
burning dusty torrential glory
and grit, imagine these thick-bodied
vultures with heads like hibiscus blooms
swept along with the scrawny cat squeezing
under the gate. The boy who survived one man
with a gun alongside the other man with a gun
who killed him. The reflection
of the crescent moon and all the windows
we've shattered with rocks and bullets and bombs.
The first new blue in two hundred years
and the gods who swallowed their children
and the gifts the sun bestowed upon all
the animals and your longing and my grief
and my longing and your grief. And maybe,
maybe, forgiveness.

Augur

Has something
winged arrived?
People wait,
fierce and wary,
on their roofs.
A few cows stand
steady, heavy
with milk.
The ground rolled,
water rose,
and now the waiting.
We don't know
that the earth's axis
tilted, bringing
more microseconds
of darkness to each
day. We do know
shattered earth,
water where
it shouldn't be,
longer nights,
waiting.
And questions:
Is the world
calling to be pillaged?

Calling for
the washing
away of names,
for bodies
to open, willingly,
everything inside
to be offered
without shame?
We need
a high priestess,
someone to read
the guts
of a strong bird,
to understand how
the ash drifts
up to the dimming,
darkening sky.

The eastern cicada killer could be called a miracle worker

For how she clasps the insects she strikes,
each cicada so rich against her belly.
She climbs a tree, flings herself
into the air, flies as far as she can before gravity
asserts itself. Then she does it again.
Her young will never see how she is
her own queen, but they will have food
for the winter when she is dead, so there's that.

She does not chant *holy holy holy*
or herald the end of the world, at least not
that we can hear. After she dies, she will not
fall from the sky as roses. Her body will decay.
But perhaps she can be the patron saint
of precious stingers and oblige
the occasional exclamation of joy or grief,
while she hums into another leap.

How could we not visit Jerusalem for Easter?

They never saw each other again, of course. Those children sat in her lap
for one leg of her journey from Beirut to Jerusalem,

their parents quick to welcome her into their car.
And that was it. They didn't cross paths with her in Boston

or San Francisco or on the road back to Beirut. She knows nothing
of the multitudes of moments they lived after they left her somewhere

between Damascus and the piles of palm leaves awaiting the believers
and the curious and the patient donkey. They still don't know about

the mother she was sure didn't love her. They didn't ask,
and she didn't offer. There was salted air to breathe and crackling

pop songs to sway to in preparation for yet another round of stories
about stones rolled away from tombs and doubt transfigured

into certainty. When their time was over, she stood
on the side of the road and waited for the next ride, closer

to taking communion that would taste like every communion
she'd ever taken. Her father was thousands of miles away

behind a locked door. Her mother was on the other side of that door.
She still believed she would never become a mother

waiting in front of a door, locked.

After reading Hemingway and Kafka while alone in my Kolkata apartment, I pour another glass of Blue Riband gin

I cut cucumber slices and dip them in salt,
because vegetables. Then I'm on the floor
watching the ceiling fan and considering
the ad's promise that Blue Riband is suitable

for parties, with a gentle suggestion
to taste it with juices instead of having it directly.
I have not added juice. The fan vibrates
warm air against warmer air.

It's too dark outside to tell the crows
on the terrace from the sky. The dogs that roam
once the sun sets sniff at the bolted door.
I hear them growling all night,

bear it just a little longer. Maybe
I'll unbolt the door. When you come home
and find me, still on the floor, huddled
with a scrawny pack of mutts, the crows keeping

watch from the armchairs, don't shout or kick
at them, don't ask if I'm ok. Just
nudge them gently to make room next
to this body. Lie down. Stay

until I can gather these bones, this
skin into something I can call my own.

How to visit someone you love in jail

That hallway.
That damn hallway.
The peeling industrial
white paint. The beautiful
wave-particle movement
of energy gone
flickering and fluorescent.
The scuffed linoleum.
The narrow windows
up against the ceiling.
So many steps. So much
time for the shrapnel
of grief to plummet
from the sky.
It's almost amazing
that I keep walking,
except that others
have walked much further.
To stop walking
would change nothing.
I will arrive
at the thick glass window.
Utilitarian chairs.
A phone.
Palms pressed
against glass.

The shrapnel buries
itself in my lungs.
The hallway
bores into
my memories
of a small boy—
over and over
again, he reaches
for my hand,
I grasp it, over
and over again.
Even when I close
my eyes, he is reaching,
and I'm grasping,
and now the shrapnel
finds my heart,
and the hallway
pushes on into
my heart,
and I am all
muscled
persistence
of blood
and breath.

I take
another step.

Listening to my students

Suddenly, rain shifts to hail, and sheaths
of water on the ground explode with each
strike of ice. Inside, we elide struggles
with faith and sons who repeat the mistakes of their fathers
and *the state can suck my dick* and
the use of space on the page and if soccer is still
the beautiful game and *I miss my brothers* and *if*
I'd known she'd die that night I would have said
I'm sorry and how to introduce a quote
and how to project your voice from your gut and black
men in chokeholds and jokes-not-jokes about
being poor mexican gay addicts
white trash living in trailers abandoned
and *I'm here look mom you didn't*
mess up our lives we've done it we've made it mother
we've won.

One of them places paper birds
all over the building. I find them tucked against
books, on top of the microwave, in desk drawers.
I don't ask who it is. I do take home
as many as I can find. Every day, I find more
until the day I don't. But that day
isn't here yet. The hail rises
to a roar against the windows. We pause
and stare at what we know of each other.
At what we don't. We wait together for
the hush I'm not quite sure will come.

Did you see the sky open when she descended?

Taking to the air with her broad body should be
impossible or at least short-lived,
but the bumblebee moves her wings
back and forth, not up and down, and hovers
on whirling dervishes of air
as I read the leaflet I just found on my car:
PUBLIC NOTICE ISSUED
Epistle to "THE DAMNED" 14 DAY NOTICE.

I don't know how many days
she has left of her roughly allotted month,
so she might be here or she might not be
when a supremely frustrated God,
cleaves the hollows under OHIO, USA,
as promised by whoever typed out
these hyper-capitalized proclamations
and attempted to evangelize me
via my windshield.
A large earthquake, buildings
and dams dashed to pieces, WATERS
BURST FORTH through GATES=FLOOD,
DESTRUCTION, DEATH=MASSIVE.
I am glad I don't live in Ohio.
Though, the writer does imply
that this damnation could reach
beyond. Either way, I am glad

this humblebee has clung, clings, will
cling until she can't anymore
to flower upon flower,
vibrating her muscles
as another blossom releases
its pollen onto her robust, furred back.

Let what must cleave, cleave:
I will not call for more sacrifices, burnt
or otherwise. I raise my open hands
to this creature as she moves above
the surface of these waters, this earth,
not as a dove or a seraphim
but as her own self, asking
for nothing except vortices of air
and open flowers.

To be mugged

Open-palmed, my heart my heart my heart.
Am I speaking politely enough, giving
enough? Will I ever get up from
this sidewalk? So many hands. None
of them my own. My pulse has never been
so loud in my throat—my spine—
my fingertips. The men leave. I cry for
my mother. Name, address, what
was taken, name, address, what was taken.
All night, someone is coming.
No one is coming. I want to get up. I want
to hold my pulse in my mouth, balance it
on my tongue, then take
the deepest breath of my life.
I want to clench my fists and feel it in my spine
strong with my own sweat, my body mine
my body mine my body mine.

When she left

—for Roberta, for my mother, for my sisters and brothers

There was so much dust in the air
as myth after myth of mother gave up
the ghost: mother as planet strong enough
to keep her moon children in orbit, mother
cultivating a garden of rooted
and sun-bent children, children saying
to mother *I want to live with you*
in the softest place, mother saying,
yes. Did her last breath come easy?
Will hers? Will ours? *Mother* flung,
a filament over teeming water,
released into glint, into gleam.

We must soberly realize that various factors exist that can lead to disharmony, insecurity, and instability

—Zhou Yonkang, Politburo member

What might you reach for with your harmonious hand?
What might roll to your feet, pique what you would not usually call

curiosity? You are too secure for that, but this does buzz a bit.
Like when you were a child and the air smelled like lightning,

or when you ran your small thumb over a tendon
and asked how it could be there every day.

Wouldn't it be lovely if it were a balloon, free but within reach.
Who wouldn't want to hold it back from the gaping sky

for just a moment, because does it somehow bear more than air?
Yes, there is some secret waiting just for you.

I have a secret, too. I am with
stirring child within a galaxy ringing

from a collision 100 million years ago
when a satellite galaxy or a dark matter halo

cast out stars. And I want to scatter the atoms of myths
layered on beeswax and bird wings

and descending gods and ascending angels and
fingers pressed to skulls and crosses on a hill

and shadows across the moon. Please, open my heart to
the expanding-for-now-universe and to your surprised hand

as you pull it back from the window, the memory
of ionized air calling to your own electricity.

Nine months pregnant on the #12 bus

He storms the #12,
black bell bottoms held up
by a spangled belt,
two sets of glasses taped together,
proclaiming over and over,
My night's just beginning!
I retreat behind my twitching
eyelids, my twitching belly—
the baby? The bus lurches
to a stop. His proclamations
diminish as he steps out.
I open my eyes as we rear back
into traffic. A woman
with horns stuck to her forehead
greets the man, *Dante! Let's go!*
And they go.

My mother still carries
the evenings when her mother
invited the priest over for dinner,
cooked fish with its head on,
put out the special china,
sat brittle and vivacious
at the head of the table,
until the priest—content
with the service of his flock—
left. And the evenings ended
as they always ended—

a woman sitting alone,
presiding over drink
after drink after drink,
as her children disappeared
upstairs.

The next stop is mine,
and I put my hands
to my spine, stand
as straight as I'm able.
I whisper to the child
within me, *there is enough
for both of us.*

Summer gardens collapse
in on themselves, leaves
yellowed, roots tapped.
I made the same thing for breakfast
today as I did yesterday.
I walk the same
uneven sidewalks,
count the same cracks, try not
to break my mother's back.
Street lights blink on.
Step after step. Step
after step. Beginning,
begin, begun.

A visitation

Crouched on the hospital bed,
I watch storm clouds scud
over the horizon. I remember
one roaming afternoon,
my shadowless child-self caught
stunned by great machines
passing over me. Then I fell, pressing
my face into the sand, afraid
of their bellies full of gleaming.

Here, now,
I hold my ground,
watch my flesh soften
and heave.

I thought it would feel
something like the rumble
of massive sharp-toothed
tools spinning out open sky
above a clear cut.
Or like an earthquake, tumbling
the stones that men in my family stacked
and hoped would always stand.

Instead, the morning
teems, falls
silent.
And then I'm holding
a small squalling being,
bare and smooth and freely
in the world, wearing the pleasure
and pain of not knowing such
tunnels of color, and my body
is all myself,
and I let out
a grassy cry.

Wikipedia defines a sound as deeper than a bight and wider than a fjord

Such homebodies, these thick-muscled harbor seals.
They only travel about five miles from where they were born
in this mountain-bound sound.
How deeply they must know their world,
with eyes fine-tuned for dark water.

And here we are, naming them, staring at them.
I think they stare back. Though as we are not refracted light,
we may be difficult for them to see. Or unnecessary.

Besides our tilted gaze,
what do we bring to this hovering morning?

That we as a species can't
agree on much, not even the shape of Earth?
It's a diamond propped up on seven pillars because
God likes the number seven. It's a flat disk under
a great dome. This is not a planet at all;
we skim across a galactic pond on a vast expanse of ice.

Not much in the way of offerings, nothing new, really.

What about descriptions of waters that are not their own?
Those shallow enough to strand a ship
or those running deep between glacier-steepened cliffs.
No need for any of that either.
They have their oxygen-rich bodies right here,
right now, and it's time—

they slip below
the light running every which way.
We can't help but step into the water, a moment
before our dense bodies remind us:
this is not ours, this brackish sanctuary.
We came onto this land, whether we call it
an oblate spheroid or a sharp-edged ruin,
and there's probably no going back.

How to survive postpartum depression

Everyone told him he
survived. He had climbed
into a full bathtub,
pulled in a toaster.
He could not believe
them. *I killed my brain.*
I can't smell. I can't
taste. I have no
thoughts,
no desire. I'm not
awake. I'm not asleep.
I have no brain.
Write the pronouns over
and over again. Talismans
of existence: He
he, he. She.
She. She. I.

He waited for the last
rhythms to cease, wandered
the local graveyard,
teeth gone black.
His brother sent the police.
Forced him to eat,
to drink, to lay down.
So on and so
forth. You're alive.
You're alive. You.

Did his brother, lifting
a spoon to that cavernous
mouth, contemplate
conceding the point?
Ferlinghetti proposed a recipe
for happiness that
included a grand boulevard
with trees, strong coffee
in small cups, and someone
who loves you. But what
do you do when
your brain only sees
death, no matter
how many leaves
shimmer in the sun?
Is there a recipe
that lets me see these
grasping hands as his
and hers and mine?

There is no one speed of sound

Folded and bent toward gathering,
they almost don't matter in the end.

However many sound waves the outer ears coax
down the dark canal at their center—

each pulse a longitudinal vein,
propelled by tension between compression

and rarefaction.
However many of those strike

the tympanic membrane into vibrations
that set three tiny bones in the middle ear

into motion. However much fluid slips
into the rooted swirled cochlea

that then bends hair cells that translate
movement into electrical impulses eager

for meaning. In the end, only the brain
can read them into sound.

And if the brain can't read
what the gentle lobes call in,

the malleus and incus and stapes could ring
forever, and her children could call her name

a million times and her world
would still drift into silence.

She wants, without hesitation,
each whisper question exclamation

footstep bark roar snap
skitter chirp cry. Each sorted

into its proper, known place. The way hummingbirds
remember every flower they visit.

Is that too much to ask? She thinks it might be,
her hands pressed against the walls of the labyrinth.

All it wants

I.

One dunlin afternoon,
her past was there.

One backlit afternoon,
her past, shy

but anguished, was there.
One finely wrought

afternoon, her past stood
there,

edges furnaced,
hemmed in burning.

One afternoon,
her past, helpless

for oxygen, sucked the air
thin and stood there,

burning. One diminishing
afternoon, her past,

bewildered, was there,
burning but didn't

ask for relief. Could
she just keep walking?

She closed her eyes, tried to
see the madonna.

II.

She closed her eyes, could
the madonna cool that heat,

make it bearable,
speak soft to the burning: I

didn't fear the angel.
I didn't fear the bold

trumpets' touch on my lips.
I wasn't afraid, no

I wasn't, no.
I didn't fear my heavy body.

The other women told
me I'd bleed.

I didn't fear my body, bleeding.
I didn't fear the waiting

angel. Don't
fear this sad,

mangled past. All it wants
you to do is say yes.

III.

All it wants
you to do is open your eyes

and say yes. All
it wants you to do

is stand still. Share a breath.
All it wants you

to do is breathe,
unclench your fists

and say yes.

I know you.

We know so little

Polistes dominula, little mistress, as you rest
in your nest with your watchful sisters and
greedy brothers, entomologists praise
how you slow down the functions of your delicate
organs tucked inside that chitinous armor,

measuring out your tightly bound life with care.
Do you admire your foundresses as you bide your time?
How they came together to claim this home,
how they knew without hesitation who would be
at the center of it all——she who has the most

scattered coloration across her regal face.
Your compound eyes stitch together thousands
of inverted queens until she is erect in front of you,
down to every twitch of her wings, which she will fold
against herself when it comes time to ride out the winter.

I have been stuck all day on our fumbling human bodies,
our meager capacity for sight, how on the clearest
of earth nights we can only see about two thousand
five hundred stars, even though for every grain
of sand on every beach on this planet

there are ten thousand stars in the universe. Are we
on the verge of being discovered, or have we already been
deemed more trouble than we're worth,
or are we spinning alone between sunrises? Of course,
whatever the answer to that question,

your young are hungry and so am I
and the universe is expanding until none
of those things are true. And there you go, casting
your bright-banded body out into the world again,
drawing on what you've saved for one more flight.

Especially when I'm afraid

My daughter tells me she dreams the dreams of wolves.
When I ask what that means, she chimes *I can never tell you.*

My mother never told me that her mother would stumble
out the door behind her in the morning, already drunk and screaming.

My mother had no mother when I was born. I wish
I could write that I always found my mother when I looked for her.

I assign myself homework: Relax my jaw, write a poem that doesn't
contain *persistent* or *gleaming*, especially when I'm afraid.

My cat needs no reminders to relax; he takes care of each part of himself
without hesitation, rough tongue to languid limbs. Then he's asleep,

quick and deep. I pass my daughter's room but don't open the door.
I hope she matches her stride to long-legged wolves

and roams, quick and deep, all night long.

My bones used to speak to me

Of honeycombed sheaths I had only known
as skin. Of loving my insatiable tongue.
How fallen and how delicious.

But now, I am in cellular silence,
and when did it become this quiet?
I think I went too long without

saying thank you for how my hard parts
hold my fleshed, quick-to-pain parts.
How many apologies do we hook

and drop into the dark of our throats?
We know how much easier it is
when we release them into

slipstreams. And yet.
I rub my hands along this scabbard of a body,
as though one more touch will coax

susurrations of marrow to the surface:
savor iron and oxygen,
quench your own thirst.

Talking about Buddhism with teenagers

There is no self. I've waited until
the very end of class to use my most
solemn teacher voice. Hands fly up:
I'm real! Is he saying
I'm not? Why would he even say that?
I remind them we are talking about a man
who fed himself to starving tigers
in one story at least.

They stare at me. The bell rings. They're gone.
I feel what I call my heart nudge
what I call my blood, like a cat demanding
touch or food or nothing at all.

I bring what I call my hands to what I call
my mouth, tender as a drunk girl
calling out, *I love your smile*
to everyone she sees.

I will never be able
to sit as straight in the moment
as a woman who parts
her hair neatly and poses for a single
photo: *for my children, after I die.*

I will never see the ocean from an ice floe,
stranded with my brothers, and cast a wooden
gaff into the water with our last words:
we lay down to perish.

What I would give to be standing in a dappled
swath of air with tigers padding toward me,
hungry and certain that I know what to do.

Advance directive

Do not insert a feeding tube. Do not attempt to resuscitate me
if I am brain dead. I initial. He initials. *Permanently Unconscious. Advanced*

Progressive Illness. Extraordinary Suffering. I sign. He signs. We are
young and healthy, but shit happens. And now it's time to discuss

what color to repaint the house next summer, what we need
from the store this afternoon. Tonight our first radiant-celled being

will order me to put my head on her chest, and she will stroke my hair.
We are so close to holding our son's nascent heart against

my heart, your heart, her heart, and damn it, I take it all back—
whatever keeps me anywhere near alive, do it.

Every last bit of whir, any scrap of murmur
and rustle, whatever churr and chirr and rush anyone can coax

from this stridulating contraption: *Do not give up*
even a single thrum. I want them all until there's nothing left.

Bargain

Dear clenching and unclenching heart:
Know that I know that I could become
a meteor shower of misfired synapses
at any time, that this frail construction

of cells will hold for a finite number of
electron leaps. But as my child gasps
himself awake—paws at me, takes
my breast in his mouth—remember, he is

your child, too. Remember his first pulse
outside of ourself, and how we caught our breath?
So tonight, let's agree that you
will receive and release blood without

fail. And I will hold our boy until
he's satisfied, his body so alive against us.

To donate: to make a gift of

A strong-winged fish might have been
the first to carry marrow in its bones.

In the company of plants discovering
their vascular nature and greening
what had been such a red planet,

alongside the still-swimming ancestors
of all of us terrestrial vertebrates,

Eusthenopteron bore its progenitor cells,
those promises of new blood,

like I do in this waiting room.
An unnamed man has a body that needs

what mine can give. Five injections of something
I can't pronounce, and my stem cells multiplied
until my larger-than-fish-bone bones weren't enough

to contain them. I sway with the force
of abundance ready to rush through
narrow plastic tubes into a machine that spins out

infinitesimal possibilities. Teeming slipstreams
for this person who wants
how much longer?

With his own body and blood
and the body and blood of his beloveds
(I hope he has beloveds) before his last breath bends?

Will my cells split into anywhere near enough
time? The needles make their way
beneath my skin. I decide the unnamed man and I are

in the Devonian oceans together,
evading shark after primitive shark, taking refuge

in the shadows of the great coral reefs, not knowing
or needing to give thanks to gravity for
keeping the water from leaving the planet,

for keeping our bodies in that water, for keeping

our bones and blood within our bodies.

I finally told my grandfather I don't believe in Jesus as God incarnate

I'm singing Christmas hymns to my son.
It's February. He's Jewish. But I know
the words, still, better even than most lullabies,
and when I'm this tired they come easy.

How he reaches for my face,
how in his world I am.
That's why I keep singing.
Though I leave out *king* for the offering

of *glory*, open my mouth wide
for *peace on earth* and *mercy mild*.
I hush *sinners*; I don't need that
hovering over either of us.

He doesn't know yet about the push pull
of atoms holding together what we call
ourselves or *sun* or *oxygen*
and really, what do I know about any of it either?

That the astronauts assure us
we glow beautifully in space, that we rotate
in some sort of reconciliation with gravity,
that I can only hold this song for so long

before it dissolves on my tongue.

What creature will hear my prayer about near misses with asteroids?

Vespa maculata will not, I'm sure.
She has no time for my perseverating
about the tenacious nature of existence;
pugnacious builder, relentless defender
of queen and egg, she is a messenger and
guardian for no one outside of her hive.
She will not carry live coals to touch
my lips and purify me; whatever
condition I am in on this marbled, burning
planet is my own business. Still, I offer

thanks that she collects leaves and bits of bark
to chew and then craft into well proportioned
hexagons, keeps her fierce face
and venomous stinger at the ready for each
of her days. She might or might not live
to see the destruction of her nest.
She might know or not know
that the chill of mid-autumn
signals the end of her time.
It probably can't hurt to add
to my calculations of our next catastrophe
a *glory*, a *hosanna* for how
she needs nothing from me
as she turns her antenna toward flowers
that perfectly fit her tongue.

Doubt

I cross the street, double back, grip
my keys between my fingers, hold
fuck you, don't touch me in my throat.

Like a frigate, a seabird that can't
dive into the ocean without drowning,
I know how to navigate my fear

for my own body. I skim, I hover,
because what else can I do?
But then I had children, and

my boy is so tender,
my girl is so fierce.
What if no matter

how many currents I find
where we can stay aloft
on our air-filled bones,

they will tire of what I want
to give them? And he decides to use
his body as a weapon,

and she becomes so quick
to please, and what if nothing
I glean from my long foraging

flights gives me a way
to keep them safe, to keep
them whole, to keep them tireless

above the open sea?

By fifth grade his son began avoiding eye contact, became increasingly fearful

—for Peter Lanza

I.

He will always be a father of a boy
who did terrible things and died without
explaining why, though
what explanation could there be.
Often his son isn't even counted
among the dead.

II.

My boy says, *No one*
can know everything. And, *You don't know*
what will happen until it happens. And, *I never*
breathe in what I breathe out and trees
keep me alive, so if when I die my soul
goes into a tree I will keep other people alive,
and I hope you're still my mother.

III.

He looked at his baby and thought,
You. We love you. I love
you. You
are precious.
Not, *One day I will regret*
that I brought you
into this world.

IV.

We offered our son reincarnation
after he started saying *I wish we weren't real*
because then we would never die,
and a quick google search brought us
to preoccupation with death at an early age
can be a sign of OCD. Such a small body
to hold so much fear, though I get it.
I really do. My body is bigger,
and here I am wondering how much
of the oxygen in my veins comes from
stars and murderers and sputtered blessings.

V.

I wish I'd looked him in the eye more.
Wish I had pulled him
against my constellation
of fear, held him so tight,
dared him to look away
from how much I love him.

My daughter, born the day an 8.9 earthquake struck Japan, calls for me

The ground shook seven times
before the quake rose one hundred and twenty miles
through mantle and ocean. Centuries

of earth-bound tension released the world
to falling. Six minutes of breaking
and stumbling and holding and holding

and fifty-four minutes later the tsunami
arrived, up to one hundred and thirty-three
feet of water. And who could let go?

But you said you were coming.
My daughter is tired of calling me,
of my casting *one moment.*

She waves to her shadow. I want to know
who was tasked with counting the one thousand
two hundred and thirty-five aftershocks.

The fifteen thousand eight hundred and fifty-four dead.
The three thousand one hundred and fifty-five missing.
Now, now? Is one moment done?

Is it? The earthquake tilted
Earth's axis by at least ten centimeters.
I swear I felt the difference when the nurse

wheeled me out the hospital door.
My daughter's shadow grows longer.
I brought her out of my darkly safe world

into this. She has stopped calling me.
Does she see a wall of water over my shoulder?
Does she feel the ground shift?

Or is it just that her ever-changing shadow
is enough for now.

A stone against your heart

Roses falling. Smoke tumbling
out of the censer at mass. Prayers folding
and diving like loons with necks
ringed in metal so they can't swallow
any fish they catch.

His thin chest. Her thick legs. His mouth
a wounded animal. Her hands
at her side like burnt stones. No one says,
I am lonely. No one
says, *I have ash in my lungs.*

She takes home dust
and calls it her child. No one says,
you could take a knife
to the throats of everyone who tells you
you're not thirsty.

The first time I give my two children a bath alone

My daughter, three years old, sturdy and brow furrowed.
My son watching what I call light and shadow, but what he calls

nothing because he is still counted in days. All I see is him
slipping into the water, her staring at me with disdain.

Raw-nippled, I can push my fists deep into my soft belly
and aching uterus. There are mothers who drive into lakes

with their babies, mothers who jump out of windows with their babies,
mothers who walk out door after door without their babies, mothers

who send their babies in baskets down rivers
to save their babies. Kneeling on the dolphin bathmat,

my hands slipping on my baby boy's slick body,
no one told me I could be one of those mothers.

Because 4,500 blackbirds fall dead from the sky when fireworks explode.
Because salt rises from once fertile fields, and what used to make kings and queens

brings men to tears as they survey all they've lost. Because scientists debate
particles that could be faster than the speed of light and violate

cause and effect, and all I want is to cover my face
and the faces of my children with wings upon wings upon wings.

I propose we worship the mud dauber

The female in particular seems worthy.
She carries mud in her jaws to make her nest
one mouthful at a time, setting up
in a crevice or a corner. One egg,
one chamber. One egg, one chamber.
It's better to keep them apart, as larvae don't
know the difference between food and a brother
or sister. They aren't wicked,
just young and hungry. She has pirate
wasps to battle—they want her young
to feed their own offspring—and she does this
alone, drinking flower nectar to keep
herself going. Let's just try

and see what happens when we raise up
this winged thing who will hover by your feet
without attacking. Covered with dense golden
hair and sometimes described as singing while
she works, all she wants is bits of damp dirt.
She has a slender thorax and two thin
sets of wings to carry her and her earth.
She is exactly strong enough
for what she needs to do. She doesn't burn
or proclaim or fill your head with visions

as she hunts crab spiders and orb
weavers and black widows. Yes, let's ask

her to pray for us as she stings
a black widow, stops its heart,
and sets off to feed her children,
singing as she holds up the world.

My conclusion is that you are worth spending time with

Agates form molecule by molecule linking
into quartz crystals beyond counting,
which then settle into clouded layers
filling pockets left by air in volcanic rock.
The agates stay their mineral-steady course
as the rock grows old and weathers away.
Eventually they tumble into the wider world.

All of this is to say, this search of ours—
backs bent, sifting handfuls
of wave-scattered stones—leaves us
wondering where the hours went. Hours,
of course, being an arbitrary measure of time,
and you know

this is what keeps me up at night.
Who decided to trap atoms,
give all their attention to shifting electrons,
count each of those oscillations
into the billions, the trillions, declaring
this is how we shall measure time?

So when you ask how
I got yet another bruise on my shin,
and I explain it's because I'm trying
to predict how many ticks we have left
on our subatomic metronome

and how many molecule-laced layers
we have room for in this pocket of space,
so I forgot to look out
for the coffee table,
I mean,
come here.

Press your mouth
to mine and I'll press
my hips to yours
and we can scatter
time-lustered breath
across each other's bodies
for hours upon
hours upon hours upon—

Finding my copy of *The Children's Book of Saints*

—for my father, as a child

In the next room, my mother drank. But she was quiet
and easy to imagine out of our world. (This was before I discovered

how heavy she was when I carried her up the stairs.)
We cut into Wonder Bread with bottle caps

to make scallop-edged communion, always took turns
as the priest and the parishioner. We had learned that some saints

went up in flames, bore wounds in the palms of their hands
that would never heal, rested atop trees as small ecstatic birds.

Together, we knew all the words to invoke and implore
and proclaim *this is my body*. Mouths soft

with sugar and flour, we consecrated ourselves.
If I knew you now, I'd tell you how one day I opened the door

and said *yes* to carrying nothing but my own self.
That we were, and are, altar enough.

All of us are dying, some just faster than others, my father says often

The way one reads ingredients aloud
from the back of the cereal box—no reason
to be angry about the lack of iron
or too much sugar or
to wish for a more complete breakfast.
There's still lunch and dinner,
and some snacks in between.

My love and I pinky promise our children we
will never divorce, and they hug us until
we almost choke, and then
they're off in a blur of ever-lengthening
legs and arms and lifelines
on their soft palms.

We argue about time:
he says it exists apart from us;
I say it's a figment of our imagination.
We don't have the inquisitive limbs
of the octopus, but even with
our dull and barely attuned bodies,
we agree the easiest solution
is to take off our clothes and stop talking.

Some comfort

Captain Underpants is on in the background
of a day made up of swans returning
to the canals of Venice and other people dying.
Of air clearing over L.A. and Tokyo
and Delhi and more people
dying. Before another day
of incident counts and recovery numbers
and so many charts and graphs that show who could

die versus who has died versus the rest of us
who could start struggling to breathe tomorrow,
as evolution granted only one way
to get oxygen into our blood for all the living
most of us want so terribly.

I try to take some comfort
that I am not *Buella frigida*—
living the rootless existence bestowed
upon all lichen while enduring
the cold-beyond-cold temperatures
and katabatic winds of the Dry Valleys of Antarctica.
But the way it subsists on water vapor and sharply

angled sunlight actually
gut-punches me with jealousy.
Because let's be honest,
our survival on this shifting substrate of stardust
is fraught on the best of days, and maybe
to be that limited and persistent would be lovely.

Or if not lovely, sufficient. Listen:
my children are laughing with big gulps
of air and take in, without
hesitation, more of what they need.
Could my own lungs ache any more?
Of course they could.

It has always been the end of times

Light curves, horizon brims,
and a bird becomes a child
bending to something shattered.
A man sobs on the shoulder of a woman or
is kissing her neck, or they are feathered
and cast shadows from broken
bits of earth. A chariot wheel
crosses the sky, pulled by photons
and bloody palms and the mothers of gods and
luminous bodies forever for never
long enough. Stand still or don't.
Name this the rotation of the celestial,
or the final uncovering, or the heart
when it comes upon the broad embrace
of a calm, dark harbor.

We all have our work to do

Three efficient cuts in my swollen abdomen.
Held together by glue and stitches
that healing will dissolve, leaving behind
thin tendrils joined to the ramified
stretch marks that remind me I'm rooted in bodies
outside of my own. Three slices into my layered
skin and fat and twined vessels of blood
by a man who cuts into what we call people
every day. I hope he does it tenderly, though
it probably doesn't matter as long as he does it
well. Watch him cut into and look inside of and take
what he needs from and then close up the body
and the body and the body every day.

We all have our work,
don't we.

A priest climbed into a plane to fly above fields
and spray holy water over what a book calls dominion.
He explained that they cleaned the pesticides out of the metal vats
before he blessed more water than he'd ever
blessed before. Watch him, the sweat soaking into his collar.
He peers into the steel drum below the belly
of the plane which, with our understanding of lift and thrust,
will leave the ground. Watch him pray for resurrection
because that one time the stone

was off to the side and the tomb was empty
except for the cloth that had been wound around
that body.

We all have our work to do, don't we.

The boys in their neat suits knock on my door, despite
the no soliciting sign. Despite the mezuzah at eye level
on the door frame. Despite the 21st century discoveries
of particles inside particles inside particles
and photographs of black holes and so many children asking
why under so many skies. Watch them stand with their perfectly aligned
name tags and their compact bibles. Watch
them believe I am ready to hear them tell me,
people will stagger from sea to sea and wander
from north to east, searching for the word of the Lord.
Watch me close the door, with all its particles firmly
in place, and return to my room, firm-footed. Watch me take
as much pleasure as I can in the work of consecrating
these always released and releasing cells we call a body.

I haven't said a Hail Mary in years

Upstairs, the couple that fights is fighting.
Next door, the dying dog howls.
His owner yells. The woman
in the apartment across the yard

moves an empty vase from
the center of the table to the end
of the table. Then back to the center.
Suppose, instead of a Marian plea

for my fellow multi-celled organisms,
I turn to *dunaliella atacamensis*, bound
with only one soft cell wall, in its cave
in the driest place on this water-heavy planet.

And I say thank you, for being
thirsty enough to take the dew
that gathers on spiderwebs first thing
in the morning and well-made enough

to live off that alone. And I bear
glad tidings to the couple and the dog
and the man who loves the dog and
the woman at her empty table

with her empty vase: thanks be
to the cave and how it opens
toward the distant Pacific Ocean,
to condensation bestowed on silken threads,

to life in a two-sided rain shadow.

Close enough

—for Hannah

One day, a dear friend calls
weeping, her father suddenly dead. One
day, we laugh about putting the kids
in front of the TV to go have hushed sex.
One day, my grandfather tells me he didn't
think he would live long enough to parent
his children. One day, he laughs as his third wife
vacuums up the spilled ashes of his first wife.
My brother is in prison. My daughter calls
herself a skunk butt. My son laughs
riotously as he blows raspberries into
the softest part of my belly. I don't know
if there's a golden mean for grief and
comedy. This feels close enough.

My dreams keep bestowing visions of my brother

One with shattered glass raining down
in a tunnel that kept narrowing. In that one,
my brother stood quiet. In that one,
I stunk with fear. I ran as the walls
hovered by my fingertips. My brother
never spoke, and I never looked
back. I saw him on the inside
of my eyelids for days.

In another, all I remembered
when I woke up
was that he had flickered
like a clusterwink snail,
blue-green and beautiful.
I still give thanks for that one.

Sometimes, all that stays with me
is the knowing that he came toward me,
a murmuration. Sometimes, the trees keen
with such insistence I know
he's crying, but he says he's fine.

I've spent some mornings certain
I left a skein of vein behind,
something I can follow the next night
to where he was when he asked me
to stay. I check my river-delta wrists
and the insides of my elbows again,
not really believing

that I'm whole. My favorite one though
by far, is when the two of us launch
ourselves down the street like long-
tendoned kangaroos, taking great leaps
until it begins to rain, real desert-nourishing
rain, and we pause together
at the end of a rustling puddle and
dip our muzzles and drink
deep. In that one, the raw voices
of my awake-world children pull
me away before I can try saying,
Peace be with you. Now leave me be.

The word *cusp* holds so many meanings

The pointed ends of the crescent moon, or the prominence
on the surface of each jaw-bound tooth, or the fold in the wall of your heart
that fills and distends if the blood flows backwards,
or wherever a curve suddenly reverses.

We could call this a cusp: how we look over our worn shoulders.

I was walking once, sure that something meant me harm,
and on an inhale, talons scraped across the top of my head.
On an exhale, the owl was in front of me, cresting
the turbulence of my heart, and on another inhale,
I was alone. The morning light ran flat, fleeting

right through me. You know what that's like, don't you.

Do you ever find your throat thickens around *and also*
with you? Maybe you become desperately thirsty
when you hear someone say, *it's witchcraft,*
someone who doesn't like me made me not myself,
because that would make more sense than any of this.

Here's what we have:

the lines of a triangle curve depending
where they are in space and sometimes
the angles will add up to more than 180 degrees.
We have seen or could be a moment away from seeing dim blue glaciers,
open caskets, gleam closing over the heads of those we love
and those we don't.
Come join us. Let's call out together for as long as it takes.

The red paper wasp as evangelist

See how she moves between nests, sometimes alone,
sometimes with her sisters. She lays her eggs, assesses
the construction of cell upon cell, keeps her options open.
And when she does finally settle, she sets to calling others
to do what they know best how to—
foraging, nest maintenance, larval care. This is what
needs to be done now if next season the new queen
is to have a chance. Stories of sinners struck dumb
and then become saved do not matter to her
construction of colonies. Neither do the pages
of pounded piths of wetland sedge
soaking up charcoal ink and promises of who
is chosen, who is not. *Polistes carolina*, she is tucked
inside *animalia*, *arthropoda*, *insecta*, *hymenoptera*,
vespidae, *polistinae*, *polistini*. None of which matters
to her either, I feel most certain. She knows what she needs
to know—that she can strike and still keep her stinger
attached to her narrow-waisted body, that she needs
to bring soft caterpillars and rich nectar back
to the larvae in her nest, that she and her sisters upon sisters

must tuck their heads toward each larva and feed them
without conflict over who begat whom. When she dies,
there is no re-telling of emperors ordering beheadings,
of miracles like water rising from the ground
where blood was spilled. No worship of small bits
of bone and cloth and incense renamed saint.
No believers caught upon the clouds together
to meet the Lord in the air. Only a barely there
exoskeleton settled to earth
and a well-fed larva closer to the promise
of a springtime queen.

Take root

We pulled up the wall-to-wall carpeting
last spring—skin cell dust,
cat pee, a million strands of hair
that choked the vacuum cleaner.
Now, the revelation of oak screeches
as I pad down the hall, and sometimes
our son stirs and our daughter calls,
but most mornings it seems my footsteps slip
through their dream lives, and yours,
as you crack your knuckles in soft-mouth sleep.

What were once forests are now beneath
my feet, and what trees will take root
someday in my own breath-empty body?

If you were awake, you wouldn't
tell me to stop thinking about death but
you'd note, perhaps, the rare discovery
of an intact planetesimal, or water ice clinging
to dust grains on the moon—something to pull
my gaze from my navel. Or maybe
you'd remind me that if I built a time machine
right now, I could go no further back
than this moment
thanks to the laws of physics
you swear are immutable.

I could live with that,
as long as I can be here
when your damp breath
pulls me down the hall,
back into bed, this morning still,
now, for a bit longer.

I close my eyes

A man and a woman sit under
this maple tree with us. There is plenty
of room and more than enough
diaphanous light. Heart-shaped seeds
settle on their shoulders, in my lap,
in my children's palms,
and I can't help but think *cathedral*.
Beneath our feet, roots tunnel and twine

and can trees ever be lonely
with such a tangle of communion?
The couple moves out into the sun,
and I want them to love each other.
My daughter chants, *Pretend*
you're dead mama, and then
wake up and be so happy
to see us. My son chimes in,
Pretend, mama, pretend.
I close my eyes to their alchemized faces.

They count
and pause and count and
pause, and I know they're
there, right there, still
there, and I'm about to gasp
Go faster! when *Open
your eyes*, they command.

I've read enough stories to know
that I should never ask
for eternity, but I would
lift up my heart to anything
that would grant us light
like forever under this tree.

It's 11:57 p.m., a bird calls over and over, and Google tries to predict my question

—for Jina

I.

What does it mean when you hear a bird at night? It could be
light beings trying to contact me. Angels can appear as birds;
are they different from light beings? Birds can be hollow-boned guides

for departed souls. There is no limit to how birds can inspire, protect,
and bring you messages of aromatic odor and a sweet burning taste
from the all-pervading medium, the subtle part

of the lower plane of existence. Or the bird might just be
doing what it can to protect its babies from what lurks in the night.
Ask the beasts, and they will teach you;

the birds of heaven, and they will tell you. Tell me what?

II.

Delta Scuti stars expand and contract hundreds of light years away from
this bird keeping the night from being too still. They probably pulsed
back when rain and hail and ice battered this bit of rotating rock

for 100 million years. They might have shone just by happenstance over
the first fungi building ever-connected branches of mycelium blooms,
and can I say that is what has held this world together despite

our human insistence on entropy? Although my husband would
interrupt here because entropy is not about us
but rather a fundamental underpinning

of the universe, *the second law of thermodynamics, the one*
that keeps me awake at night, he would say. Then I would kiss him
because I'm the one in this relationship who is supposed to carry

the existential distress, not him. The bird is quiet now.

III.
And still, my breath is loud. And still, what does it mean to listen?
And still, the fungi are here, ensuring that the birch knows
when the smoke bush is thirsty so it can share some water,

checking on the cherry tree and its fruiting,
winding among the curious roots of the Douglas fir just beginning,
reminding the oak it's never alone.

We are visitors in their kingdom. Along with whatever being,
light or winged or otherwise, made itself known tonight. I hum to all of us,
What else can we tell each other? I'm listening. Promise.

If the manufacturer's promise holds true, the new roof will outlast my father

And he admires that probability. It's far more likely
than the chance of us being here as who we are; someone calculated that
as about 400 trillion to one. He admires this, too, and how the sun

sits on our shoulders right now. Under the eaves of that sturdy-as-hell roof,
the common ariel hornet tucked her nest for the summer.
I was about to describe the season as brief,

but that is only how my stuttering synapses
process time. So, I assure myself that my father will live damn close
to forever, with a quick sidestep to knock on the closest tree and shush

any wisp of a god still hovering nearby. The bit of sun moves,
so we move. *Dolichovespula arenaria* probably notes
where our ungainly grounded bodies take up space

and keeps a safe distance, her stinger at the ready but sheathed
as long as we don't keep her from the lacewings and spiders
she seeks for her still-soft larvae. The larvae trust her strong mandibles

will bring back what they need, and she trusts
the secreted sugar they offer back when they're full,
a nectar of thanks that offers the sisterhood another shot

at another summer day. Again, the sun shifts. And there's so much
light striking my ever-blinking eyes that it's hard to bear
witness to much beyond my warm shoulders, beyond the idea

of my father next to me, beyond the communion of chance.

My work has always been

—for Bear and Emma

To fall in love
with my sisters' faces while
they sing. My heart catching
on all their hearts.
To keep singing
as men with all the killing steel gather
at the darkening horizon.
To sing *abundance* and *the blade*
and *let's take each other*
in our arms. To have the men burn
us to the ground.
To fall in love with the ground.

To gather with the oak trees
along the river bottom, where my sisters
and I do unto ourselves
in the sweet grasses.
To know stars
will not descend to banish the men
who whisper that we are devil-bound.
To gather anyway:
my rooted body,
her ascending body,
our overflowing body.

To keep my sisters in my pulse
when the men bring me to sit where

the earth trembles sometimes.
Which scares them
and pleases me. To say nothing
when they give me the rotting
names of monsters slain by gods.
To call vapor into prophecy
the men will never understand:
*yes, you are no more
than burnt skin and bone.*

To love my own name,
our own singing names,
to love every single one of us

going up in smoke.

Tumble

—for my children

Here I never shush my body. See
the light on my shoulders, on my head? Crowned,
I rustle through ferns like water, step
onto the stone wall, follow it into
the woods where no one can ever find me,
unless I want them to. Tender mosses,
lustrous deer skulls, fierce trees
with muscled limbs—all of them keep my secrets
safe. I can trick you so you think
a rock is just a rock. A rock is never
just a rock. Listen to all the promises
this loamed earth offers. Be not
afraid. We are never going back.

My daughter asks me about her breast buds, and I don't want to fuck this up because what if they had told me that this is what a body can do and it's beauty?

You don't need to praise anything other than
these warm, sticky cells on the most tender part
of your thighs. Lay down with your own
loving hands and touch the blood on
your sheets when you're done. Then any ghost
on the edge of the room will know you're not afraid
and not worth haunting. You are not
a clenched mouth, or a crackling spine,
or a weeping rib, or any of the other parts
they want for themselves. You are clouds
shadowed and unshadowed so quickly
my head spins. Listen for what
could be insects casting their bodies into air,
or seed pods bursting open. Look
for the doe who has tucked herself under
the low, glowing branches of an apple tree
in this wing-brimmed meadow. You
are dusk and dust and deserving.

Notes

Page 41, "We know so little": The questions of "who is watching us? Is there any life elsewhere in the universe that observes us?" are what scientists describe as poorly constrained problems. They do not have enough parameters to truly investigate because we know so little.

Page 34, "How to Survive Postpartum Depression": Some references are from a *New Scientist* article on 23 May 2013 by Helen Thomson.

Page 26, "We must soberly realize that various factors exist which can lead to disharmony, insecurity, and instability": From a statement issued by the head of Chinese security forces before a Communist Party Congress in 2012. The government ordered taxi drivers to lock their cab doors and disable windows to prevent passengers from reaching for bouncing ping pong balls or drifting balloons that could carry messages of revolution.

Page 55, "By fifth grade his son began avoiding eye contact, became increasingly fearful": After reading "The Reckoning" by Andrew Solomon in the March 17, 2014 issue of the *New Yorker*. The article ends with this quote: "Peter declared that he wished Adam had never been born, that there could be no remembering who he was outside of who he became. 'That didn't come right away. That's not a natural thing, when you're thinking about your kid. But, God, there's no question. There can only be one conclusion, when you finally get there. That's fairly recent, too, but that's totally where I am.'"

Acknowledgments

Versions of these poems have appeared or are forthcoming
in the following magazines:

Euphony Journal: "Tumble"

JMWW: "How to Survive Postpartum Depression," "A Visitation,"
    "How to Be Mugged"

New Haven Review: "Nine Months Pregnant on the #12 Bus"

New Ohio Review: "I propose we worship the mud dauber," "If the
    manufacter's promise holds true"

Nimrod International Journal of Prose and Poetry: "We all have our work
    to do," "Especially When I'm Afraid," "After reading Hemingway and
    Kafka while alone in my Kolkata apartment, I pour another glass of
    Blue Riband gin," "Some comfort," "Finding my copy of *The Children's
    Book of Saints*," "Talking about Buddhism with teenagers," and "To
    donate: to make a gift of"

Northwest Review: "All it wants" (was "Witness")

Painted Bride: "Augur"

Tar River Poetry: "Close Enough"

The Madison Review: "How to Visit Someone You Love in Jail"

Timberline Review: "Listening to my students"

To Shane and Noah, greeting the day with you is a gift. Thank you for wandering and wondering and loving with me.

To Bear, Emma, and Heather, for your loving laughing healing company.

To my parents, who bought me my first journal, and my second, and my third.

To my Papa, for introducing me to Gerard Manley Hopkins.

To my Grandma, for coming into this family and bringing the best hugs.

To my writer/artist sisters, Hannah, Jina and Nichole, because of course.

To Mrs. Ryan, who helped me publish my first poem in fifth grade.

To my village, near and far. What a gift to be connected to and in community with so many creative, generous, loving, hilarious accumulations of star dust.

To all of my teachers, especially the young people I've worked with over the years. What an honor to know you and learn with you.

A Pushcart Prize and Best New Poets
nominee, **JESSICA PIERCE** has poems
in magazines including *CALYX Journal*,
Bellingham Review, *Tar River Poetry*,
Euphony, and *Painted Bride Quarterly*.
Nimrod International Journal selected
her as a finalist for the 2020 Pablo
Neruda Prize for Poetry. She was a
finalist in the 2020 Lois Cranston
Memorial Poetry Prize from *CALYX
Journal*, a finalist in *New Ohio Review*'s
2019 NORward Prize for Poetry, a
finalist in the 2019 MVICW Poetry
Contest, and the recipient of a 2019
MVICW Poet Fellowship.

FIRSTMATTERPRESS
Portland, Ore.

SELECTED TITLES FROM FIRST MATTER PRESS

BODY UNTIL LIGHT
K.M. Lighthouse

CONSIDER THE BODY, WINGED
Jessica E. Pierce

IT'S JUST YOU & ME, MISS MOON
Emily Moon

LOVERS AND OTHER STILL CREATURES
Eitan Codish

OTHERWISE, MAGIC
Lauren Paredes

ROUTES BETWEEN RAINDROPS
Dan Wiencek

THE GROWTH LINES
Gabby Hancher

THE NIGHT SKY IS A PLACE WHERE THINGS GET LOST
Andrew Chenevert

WE ARE NOT READY FOR WHAT WE ARE
Ash Good

FIRSTMATTERPRESS.ORG